Thank You for
the Little Things

Thank You for the Little Things

It Is All About Perspective

dLee

www.themightymuser.com

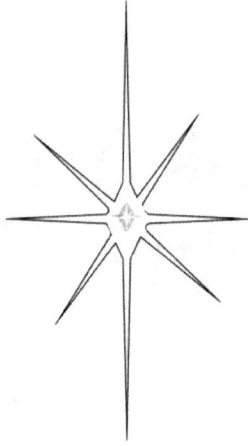

This book is dedicated with heartfelt appreciation to the people who have had a profound effect on me throughout my creative lifetime. I sincerely appreciate Lynn Scheurell (The Creative Catalyst) and Sandra Rodgers (Network Director, VoiceAmerica Talk Radio) who have been a steady source of guidance, inspiration and encouragement.

Thank you!

"The creative is the place where no one else has ever been. You have to leave the city of your comfort and go into the wilderness of your intuition. What you'll discover will be wonderful. What you'll discover is yourself."
~ Alan Alda

"Gratitude opens the door to ... the power, the wisdom, the creativity of the universe. You open the door through gratitude."
~ Deepak Chopra

Introduction

If you want to make a change, shift into a different mindset, or cultivate a passion, you must let go of your busyness and make time for reflection.

Most likely, you are searching outside of yourself for inspiration. In the past, a guiding source was referred to as a muse. The muse was a person who inspired a creative response or action. In actuality, the best muse is within yourself.

We all live busy and noisy lives. Some people go out of their way to avoid quiet moments, when they are not busy or lacking in distractions. These people will likely forget to be thankful.

Inner peace and being present in the moment might seem as elusive as chasing a rainbow. Wake up and disengage for a moment. Actively create time every day for yourself—to simply pause from all of the demands on your time and attention.

This book is meant to be a tool you can use to capture your thoughts and musings as you explore your wonderful inner beingness. Ponder the quotes within and find inspiration and solutions to your daily challenges by listening to your heart and soul. As you write your musings, you might experience a spiritual moment that results in inspiration to open your heart. You might also receive insight for action.

Try an attitude of curiosity and discovery; look for moments to play, to be thankful, and to be wonder-filled in awe. Make the choice to simply connect by using all of your senses. Feel the breeze on your face, listen to Mother Nature's sounds, and take a close look at a colorful sky.

There is no right or wrong way to approach making time for yourself to write. How you choose to use the 86,400 seconds you have each day is a personal choice. Usually the greatest challenge is to make time for writing and finding your style.

All of your daily moments are precious. Take a close look at how you spend yours as there are possible moments buried within your busy schedule and each moment can be a treasure. By paying attention, you can take advantage of "free" moments while you are waiting in line, stopped at a stop sign, sitting on the bus, etc. Take a breath, pause, and pay attention to how you feel with whatever you are doing ... it can be as simple as savoring a single bite of food during a meal.

Savor each moment.

You are the hero of your own story. Your discoveries and conclusions are unique, as you creatively explore your observations and insights.

Add Color to Your Musings

Sprinkled throughout the pages are a variety of black-and-white images you can add color to as you are musing. Color outside of the lines. How does it feel? Coloring, a favorite pasttime for generations, is proven to help reduce stress.

Try it!

"So you see, imagination needs moodling—long, inefficient, happy idling, dawdling and puttering."
~ Brenda Ueland

"The most potent muse of all is our own inner child."
~ Stephen Nachmanovitch

What If ...

You look around
Without a sound
A shared smile will flow for miles
You immerse yourself in nature's colors
You feel a spark of appreciation
For the simple way it is just there
What if you really care
You pick up something dropped and out of place
You put it away somewhere
You hear the chirp of a bird in a tree
You feel a spark of appreciation
For the simple way it is just there
What if everyone would express a thought of joy
Where does it lead
Where is the peace
Where is the release
What if a valued minute is spent by everyone
With passion
With gratitude
In friendship
In tranquility
With courage
In prosperity
We would all become a catalyst
To change our little world!

~ dLee

This is *Your* Journey

1. Pick a time of day when you are alert and can be uninterrupted. Test out different times to find out which works best.

2. Find a cozy spot where you can have a few minutes of peace and quiet.

3. Clear your mind. Breathe deeply. These basic steps will quiet your inner being and open you for making a solid connection to your soul.

4. Flip through this book and pick one quote to muse about. Ask yourself thought-provoking questions as you ponder the topic and pay attention as you listen to your responses—you might get answers that you enjoy.

5. Focus on your breath and sense your thoughts coming in; and then allow them to leave.

6. In the space provided, write down any musings you notice on the little things you want to save and explore later.

7. Let go and allow. As you give yourself time to disengage, you will likely begin to get thoughts and receive answers to your questions.

My Musings ...

A little "thank you" that you will say to someone for a "little favour" shown to you is a key to unlock the doors that hide unseen "greater favours." Learn to say "thank you" and why not?

~ Israelmore Ayivor

My Musings ...

You need to let the little things that would ordinarily bore you suddenly thrill you.
~ Andy Warhol

_____

_____

_____

_____

_____

_____

_____

_____

_____

_____

_____

_____

_____

_____

_____

_____

_____

_____

My Musings ...

The small things of life were often so much bigger than the great things ... the trivial pleasures like cooking; one's home; little poems, especially sad ones; solitary walks; funny things seen and overheard.
~ Barbara Pym

My Musings ...

No person, no place, and no thing has any power over us, for we are the only thinkers in our mind. When we create peace and harmony and balance in our minds, we will find it in our lives.

~ Louise L. Hay

My Musings ...

Sometimes the little opportunities that fly at us each day can have the biggest impact.
~ Danny Wallace

My Musings ...

What you repeatedly do carries the clay to mold you into who you eventually become. Don't despise any tiny minute of the day; each counts so much!

~ Israelmore Ayivor

My Musings ...

The golden opportunity you are seeking is in yourself. It is not in your environment, it is not in luck or chance, or the help of others; it is in yourself alone.

~ Orison Swett Marden

My Musings ...

Without water drops, there can be no oceans;
without steps, there can be no stairs; without
little things, there can be no big things!
~ Mehmet Murat ildan

My Musings ...

Find magic in the little things, and the big things you always expected will start to show up.

~ Isa Zapata

_____

_____

_____

_____

_____

_____

_____

_____

_____

_____

_____

_____

_____

_____

_____

_____

_____

_____

My Musings ...

It's only when the clock is ticking all those little things add up and become bigger.
~ Shannon Wiersbitzky

My Musings ...

Great ideas emerge from useless fragments
of thoughts.
~ Michael Bassey Johnson

My Musings ...

Find gratitude in the little things and your
well of gratitude will never run dry.
~ Antonia Montoya

My Musings ...

No matter how small the effort is, if done consistently, it will start compounding and before you know it, you would have already realized your dream.
~ Zeeshan Raza

My Musings ...

Do the little things. In the future when you look back, they'd have made the greatest change.

~ Nike Thaddeus

My Musings ...

It probably wouldn't last. It never does. But it would come back around again. That's how life works. And that's why it's important to treasure the peaceful times—so you can persevere through the other kind.
~ Jean Ferris

My Musings ...

Watch the little things; a small leak will sink a great ship.
~ Benjamin Franklin

My Musings ...

Never get tired of doing little things for others. Sometimes those little things occupy the biggest part of their hearts.
~ Unknown

My Musings ...

The way we do small things determines the way we do everything.
~ Robin Sharma

_____

_____

_____

_____

_____

_____

_____

_____

_____

_____

_____

_____

_____

_____

_____

_____

_____

My Musings ...

Not all of us can do great things. But we can do small things with great love.
~ Mother Teresa

My Musings ...

Work to connect yourself to the allness of life —instead of identifying with the smallness of it—and you'll awaken to a greatness already living within you that is no more bothered by the little things in life than a mountain is made miserable by rain that falls upon it.
~ Guy Finley

My Musings ...

The blind only wish to see, the deaf only wish to hear and the mute only wish to speak. Things that seem of just little value to us, can be ALL that someone else wants ... appreciate even the little things in life ... many are less fortunate.
~ Unknown

My Musings ...

Life is made up, not of great sacrifices or duties, but of little things, in which smiles, and kindnesses, and small obligations, given habitually, are what win and preserve the heart and secure comfort.
~ Humphrey Davy

My Musings ...

It's a hard world for little things.
~ Davis Grubb

My Musings ...

Sometimes the smallest things take up the most room in your heart.
~ Winnie the Pooh

My Musings ...

Your inner strength is your outer foundation.
~ Allan Rufus

My Musings ...

Embrace the power of little things and you will build a tower of mighty things. Mighty things are made up of varieties of little things put together.

~ Israelmore Ayivor

_____

_____

_____

_____

_____

_____

_____

_____

_____

_____

_____

_____

_____

_____

_____

_____

_____

_____

My Musings ...

Dust is the parent of a star!
~ Munia Khan

_____
_____
_____
_____
_____
_____
_____
_____
_____
_____
_____
_____
_____
_____
_____
_____
_____
_____
_____

My Musings ...

Big things hit you in the face with their big-
ness and obscure the little, more important
things that really define a life and provide it
with delicacy.
~ Lauren Roedy Vaughn

My Musings ...

Never let the little things, disrupt the biggest things you cherish in life. The smallest mistake, can cause the biggest regret and hurt to your closest companion.

~ Unarine Ramaru

My Musings ...

There is no such thing as the pursuit of happiness, but there is the discovery of joy.
~ Joyce Grenfell

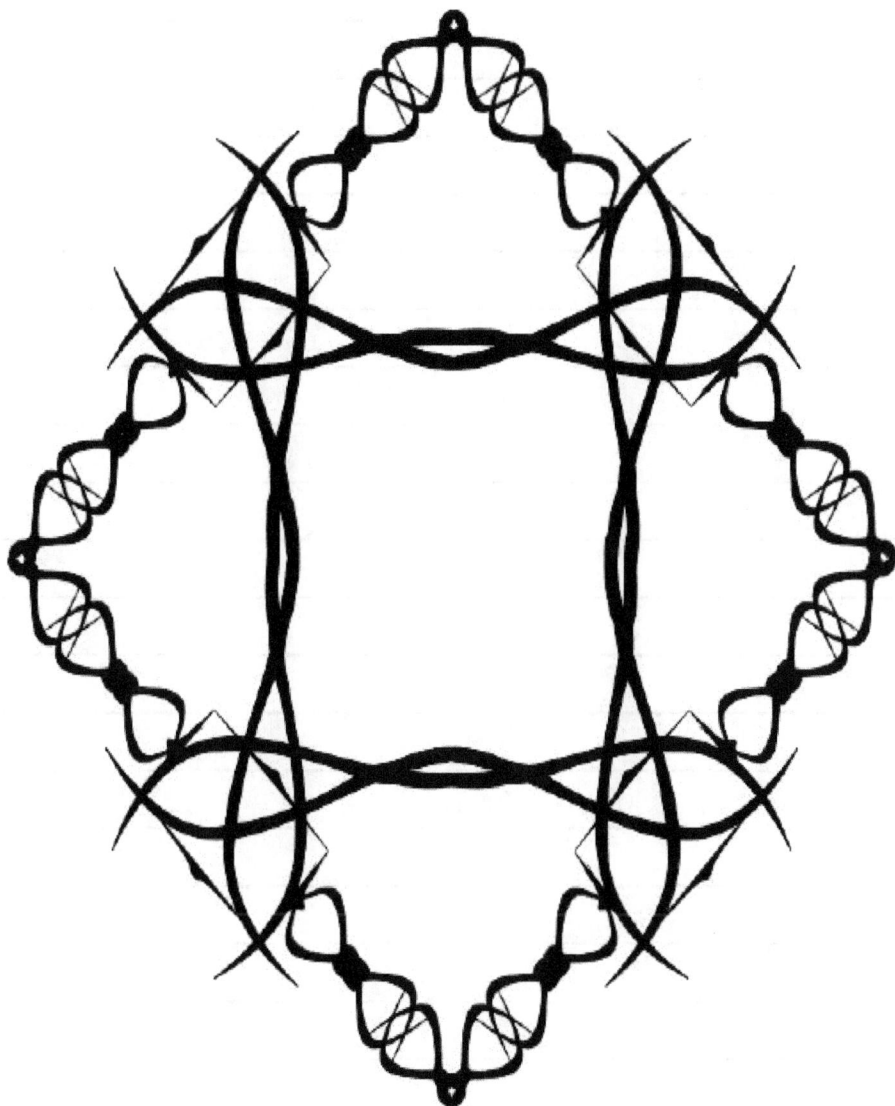

My Musings ...

No matter how small the effort is, if done consistently, it will start compounding and before you know it, you would have already realized your dream.

~ Zeeshan Raza

My Musings ...

He who does not wish for little things does not deserve big things.
~ Belgian Proverb

My Musings ...

Sometimes it's the same moments that take your breath away that breathe purpose and love back into your life.
~ Steve Maraboli

My Musings ...

Every day we have plenty of opportunities to get angry, stressed or offended. But what you're doing when you indulge these negative emotions is giving something outside yourself power over your happiness. You can choose to not let little things upset you.
~ Joel Osteen

My Musings ...

In the sweetness of friendship let there be laughter, and sharing of pleasures. For in the dew of little things the heart finds its morning and is refreshed.
~ Khalil Gibran

My Musings ...

Sometimes the most happy people in life are the ones with nothing. We can't lose sight of the little things in life that should make us the happiest.

~ Ryan Cabrera

My Musings ...

Sometimes when I consider what tremendous consequences come from little things, I am tempted to think there are no little things.
~ Bruce Barton

My Musings ...

I don't look to jump over seven-foot bars; I look around for one-foot bars that I can step over.

~ Warren Buffett

My Musings ...

It can be helpful simply to make a written or mental list of the things you do each day. Then give yourself a mental credit for each of them, however small. This will help you focus on what you have done instead of what you haven't gotten around to do. It may sound simplistic, but it works.
~ David D. Burns

My Musings ...

A mighty flame followeth a tiny spark.
~ Dante Alighieri

My Musings ...

The happiness of life is made up of minute fractions—the little, soon-forgotten charities of a kiss or smile; a kind look; a heartfelt compliment; and the countless infinitesimal of pleasurable and genial feeling.
~ Samuel Taylor Coleridger

My Musings …

It is in these acts called trivialities that the seeds of joy are forever wasted, until men and women look round with haggard faces at the devastation their own waste has made, and say, the earth bears no harvest of sweetness—calling their denial knowledge.
~ George Eliot

My Musings ...

The person determined to achieve maximum success learns the principle that progress is made one step at a time. A house is built one brick at a time. Football games are won a play at a time. A department store grows bigger one customer at a time. Every big accomplishment is a series of little accomplishments.

~ Dr. David Schwartz

My Musings ...

The thing that goes the furthest towards making life worthwhile, that costs the least, and does the most, is just a pleasant smile.
~ Wilbur D. Nesbit

My Musings ...

A mountain is composed of tiny grains of earth. The ocean is made up of tiny drops of water. Even so, life is but an endless series of little details, actions, speeches, and thoughts. And the consequences whether good or bad of even the least of them are far-reaching.

~ Sri Swami Sivananda

My Musings ...

Inch by inch, it's a cinch.
~ Robert H. Schuller

My Musings ...

People often say that this or that person has not yet found himself. But the self is not something that one finds. It is something that one creates.

~ Thomas Szasz

My Musings ...

Explore your mind, discover yourself, then give the best that is in you to your age and to your world. There are heroic possibilities waiting to be discovered in every person.
~ Wilfred Peterson

My Musings ...

Journey from the self to the Self and find the mine of gold. Leave behind what is sour and bitter and move toward the sweet.
~ Rumi

My Musings ...

Explore. All life is an experiment. The more experiments you make, the better.
~ Ralph Waldo Emerson

My Musings ...

Heroes take journeys, confront dragons, and discover the treasure of their true selves.
~ Carol Pearson

My Musings ...

Try to put well into practice what you already know. In so doing, you will, in good time, discover the hidden things you now inquire about.

~ Rembrandt

My Musings ...

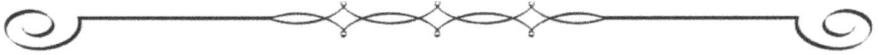

We don't receive wisdom; we must discover
it for ourselves after a journey that no one
can take for us or spare us.
~ Marcel Proust

My Musings ...

A leader will find it difficult to articulate a coherent vision unless it expresses his core values, his basic identity ... one must first embark on the formidable journey of self-discovery in order to create a vision with authentic soul.

~ Mihaly Csikszentmihalyi

My Musings ...

The most important encounter in life is the encounter with oneself.
~ Yves Saint Laurent

My Musings ...

Art is not just ornamental, an enhancement of life. It is a path in itself, a way out of the predictable and conventional ... a map to self-discovery.

~ Gabrielle Roth

My Musings ...

A journey is only as interesting as the secret of its detail.

~ Aj Leal

My Musings ...

I think somehow we learn who we really are
and then we live with that decision.
~ Eleanor Roosevelt

My Musings ...

Ninety percent of the world's woe comes from people not knowing themselves, their abilities, their frailties, and even their real virtues. Most of us go almost all the way through life as complete strangers to ourselves—so how can we know anyone else?

~ Sidney J. Harris

My Musings ...

One must know oneself. If this does not
serve to discover truth, it at least serves as
a rule of life and there is nothing better.
~ Blaise Pascal

My Musings ...

People acting in their own self-interest is the fuel for all the discovery, innovation, and prosperity that powers the world.
~ John Stossell

My Musings ...

To be calm and compassionate you need courage and conviction.
~ Solange Nicole

My Musings ...

Wandering is the activity of the child, the passion of the genius; it is the discovery of the self, the discovery of the outside world, and the learning of how the self is both "at one with" and "separate from" the outside world. These discoveries are as fundamental to the soul as "learning to survive" is fundamental to the body. These discoveries are essential to realizing what it means to be human. To wander is to be alive.

~ Roman Payne

My Musings ...

At the center of your being you have the answer; you know who you are and you know what you want.
~ Lao Tzu

My Musings ...

One must still have chaos in oneself to be able to give birth to a dancing star.
~ Friedrich Nietzsche

My Musings ...

Dig within. Within is the wellspring of Good; and it is always ready to bubble up, if you just dig.

~ Marcus Aurelius

My Musings ...

We shall not cease from exploration and the end of all our exploring will be to arrive where we started and know the place for the first time.

~ T. S. Eliot

My Musings ...

The only journey is the one within.
~ Rainer Maria Rilk

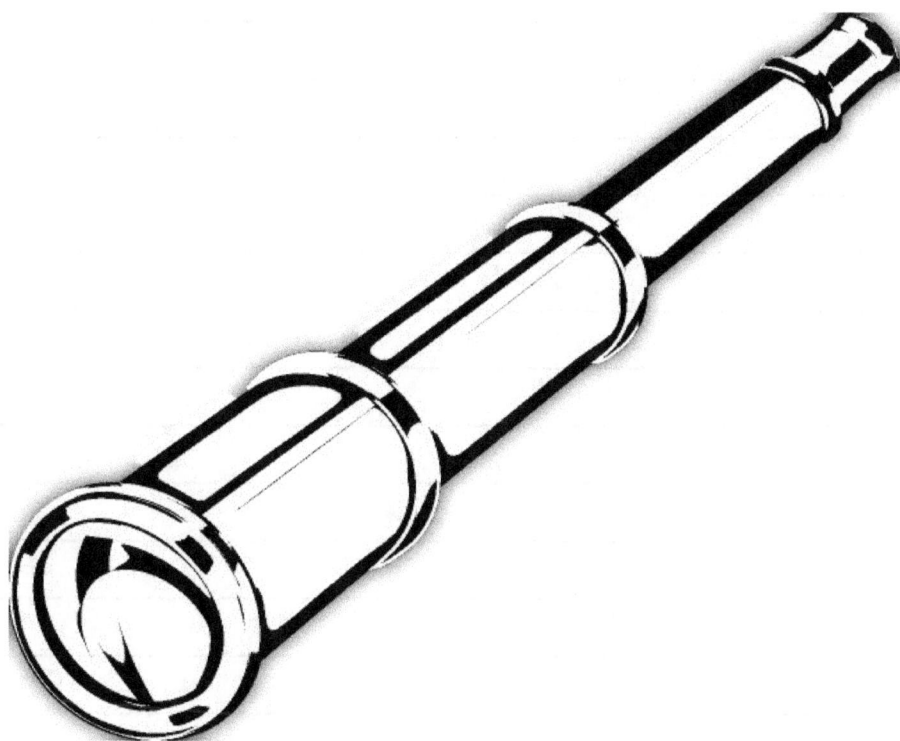

My Musings ...

It does not matter how long you are spending on the earth, how much money you have gathered or how much attention you have received. It is the amount of positive vibration you have radiated in life that matters.
~ Amit Ray

My Musings ...

If you get the inside right, the outside will fall into place. Primary reality is within; secondary reality without.

~ Eckhart Tolle

My Musings ...

Your inner strength is your outer foundation.
~ Allan Rufus

_____

_____

_____

_____

_____

_____

_____

_____

_____

_____

_____

_____

_____

_____

_____

_____

_____

_____

My Musings ...

It's daring to be curious about the unknown, to dream big dreams, to live outside pre-scribed boxes, to take risks, and above all, daring to investigate the way we live until we discover the deepest treasured purpose of why we are here.

~ Luci Swindoll

My Musings ...

If you begin to understand what you are without trying to change it, then what you are undergoes a transformation.
~ Jiddu Krishnamurti

My Musings ...

In wisdom gathered over time I have found
that every experience is a form of exploration.
~ Ansel Adams

My Musings ...

A classic is a book which with each rereading offers as much of a sense of discovery as the first reading.
~ Italo Calvino

My Musings ...

I make a discovery in a poem as I write it.
~ Rita Dove

My Musings ...

With time, many of the facts I learned were forgotten but I never lost the excitement of discovery.

~ Paul Berg

My Musings ...

The greatest discovery of my generation is that human beings can alter their lives by altering their attitudes of mind.
~ Lee Iacocca

My Musings ...

We often discover what will do, by finding out what will not do; and probably he who never made a mistake never made a discovery.
~ Samuel Smiles

My Musings …

What lies behind you and what lies in front of you, pales in comparison to what lies inside of you.

~ Ralph Waldo Emerson

_____

_____

_____

_____

_____

_____

_____

_____

_____

_____

_____

_____

_____

_____

_____

_____

_____

"Success in life is founded upon attention to the small things rather than to the large things; to the everyday things nearest to us rather than to the things that are remote and uncommon."
~ Booker T. Washington

A *Secret* Little Thing is Waiting for You!

It is a nice gesture to send notes of appreciation whenever possible. The secret to staying on top of this almost-forgotten courtesy is having the necessary supplies. When you have everything in one place (paper, envelopes, and pen), you can simply act whenever you think of sending a thank-you note.

Get your *Thank You for Little Things Station* instructions so you are organized. When you want to write a thank-you note, you will have all of the critical supplies handy.

Claim your special free gift at this hidden page:

www.mightygems.com/TYS

The real gems of life are good deeds, special people, and stories of our humanity. The spotlight merely illuminates the ordinary preciousness contained within our daily lives. By spotlighting everyday jewels, we learn to see them together ... and that's the real treasure.

Check out our radio show, "Mighty Gems: Spotlighting Everyday Jewels in Life," which airs weekly on Fridays at 11am PST/2pm EST on VoiceAmerica Internet Radio as part of their Empowerment Channel at www.voiceamerica.com.

About the Author

dLee is a lifelong "Muser." A great deal of her life has been spent spinning life happenings into positivity.

Starting at a very young age, dLee thought a little differently than everyone else. She wrote poetry, played with words, and liked math. It seemed she was always going beneath the surface of events to tap into the inspiration in them, looking for greater happiness and joy.

dLee always looked on the bright side and used that as a way to stay open to life's experiences. It's not easy to do as a child—she heard "Pollyanna" a lot—but now people tell her it's a sign of enlightenment. She knows that life is about feeling good, taking inspired action, and living larger than you might imagine through creativity. It is also being grounded in foundational concepts.

dLee spends her days balancing creative inspiration with the practical side of running a small business, spending precious time with family and friends, while following her passions and expanding ingenuity as a way of life.

From the top of each day
Align yourself first as number one.
With your daily precious time
Connect directly within.
Your day will gracefully begin
And flow smoothly until your evening hour ends.
~ dLee

9 780996 798303